# I CHOOSE
# to Be Me

I CHOOSE SERIES

ELIZABETH ESTRADA

Copyright 2022 by Elizabeth Estrada - All rights reserved.
Published and printed in the USA.

No part of this publication or the information in it may be quoted or reproduced in any form by means of printing, scanning, photocopying, or otherwise without permission of the copyright holder.

# I CHOOSE
# to Be Me

ELIZABETH ESTRADA

I choose to be me,
I like who I am inside.
When I think of my best qualities,
I really do feel pride.

I am brave and adventurous,
And don't mind the hard path.
I am goal-oriented and driven,
I strive to stay on track.

I am kind to other people,
I go out of my way to help them out.
When someone says they need help,
I'm there without a second doubt.

I am a thoughtful daughter,
And considerate of my family.
I know my heritage and culture
Are important parts of what make me me.

I know what's in my heart
That is most important of all,
Not whether I'm heavy or thin,
Short or tall.

I'm confident in how I look
That I was created as I should be.
I like that there is no one else out there
Who looks exactly like me.

I like to dress in my own style,
Even if my clothes make me stand out in a crowd.
Representing my own style
Is something that makes me proud.

I try my best at sports,
And I give each one a chance.
I work hard at practice,
So that I may advance.

If I make a bad grade,
I know it will be fine.
I don't fret, instead I study harder,
So that I can do better next time.

I am not the most social,
Sometimes I feel a little shy.
But when there is a new student,
I always reach out and say "hi."

It makes me happy that I have friends,
A few who are always by my side.
I know no matter what I'm going through,
They will help me get through it in stride.

Sometimes, when I disagree with something,
I speak up about what's on my mind.
I always advocate for those less fortunate,
In a way that is respectful and kind.

I also stand up for others,
When I feel they are being treated wrong.
I speak up and say something.
When I do this, I feel strong.

I like to share my opinions,
And also listen to the opposite side.
I try to get all the information,
Before I finally decide.

I know that I have lots to offer,
As a person and a friend.
When I am authentic,
I don't need to pretend.

I like to make others laugh,
And show off my creativity in my art.
I have talents and skills
That I know set me apart.

I love being who I am,
And competing tasks to the end.
I love to meet others who accept me,
And welcome them as my friends.

I choose to be me,
And to be confident in my own skin.
I consider being born as me
The ultimate win!

www.ingramcontent.com/pod-product-compliance
Lightning Source LLC
Chambersburg PA
CBHW041524070526
44585CB00002B/72